Colorful Cities
Seattle, Washington
www.colorfulcities.com | info@colorfulcities.com

100% designed, illustrated and printed in the United States of America.

ISBN: 978-0-9898972-6-6
Library of Congress Control Number: 2022921939

Concept, Design & Text: Laura Lahm
Art Direction: Jenna Ashley
All Illustrations by Steph Calvert with the exception of numbers 6, 19, 20, 24, 31, 33 which were illustrated by Retsu Takahashi

For more cities in the Explore & Color series please visit colorfulcities.com

A few great ways to *Explore & Color* Seattle, whether you're in the city or at home!

- Create a contest to explore as many of Colorful Seattle's locations as possible.

- Count how many waterways you go over as you explore the city.

- Page Roulette! Turn to a random page and let the illustration be your starting point to explore or color.

- Build a scavenger hunt based on the illustrations.

- Ride your bike along the Burke-Gilman Trail and stop to color along the way.

- Drop your pencil on the map and explore the nearest location to your landing point or color that illustration.

- Use the map and index to plan an itinerary based upon your favorite illustrations.

- Try to find the statue of the guitarist who wrote, sang, and played "Purple Haze" on his guitar in 1967.

- Be green and see how many locations you can visit by only using public transportation—Link Light Rail, city bus, or your feet!

- Color the Duwamish Longhouse illustration then learn the history of the Coast Salish People.

- Make art for your walls. Perforations at the top of the pages make this easy to do!

Get Ready to Explore Seattle!

Located in the Pacific Northwest along the Puget Sound, Seattle is commonly known for its coffee culture, music scene, and for its technology behemoths; great influences that have helped define this city. Yet what is metropolitan Seattle today, was formerly land belonging to the Coast Salish people, namely, the Suquamish and Duwamish Tribes. The name "Seattle" is actually a derivative of Chief Si'ahl (pronounced "See-ahlth"), the leader of both tribes at the time the first settlers arrived here in 1851.

Seattle's uniqueness can be chalked up to some great numbers. 605 feet is the height of the iconic Space Needle which towered over the 1962 World's Fair and remains an intrinsic component of the skyline today. 80,000 is the number of salmon which travel through the neighborhood of Ballard in a series of fish ladders that assist them in reaching inland streams for spawning every spring. 485 public parks dot the city providing green space year-round for residents and visitors, alike. 148 miles of freshwater coast extend along Lake Union and Lake Washington, while the Puget Sound, which leads to the Pacific Ocean, defines the city's western edge. 2 mountain ranges, the Cascades to the east and the Olympics to the West, bookend city views, and 1 volcano, Mount Rainier, makes occasional appearances, depending on its mood (and the weather). Frequently you'll hear locals asking, "Is the mountain out today?".

With so many sights to see it can be hard to decide where to begin, but don't worry, we've got a few tried and true ideas for you as you embark on your exploration of this magnificent city:

- Historic sculptures pepper various neighborhoods – the not-so-hidden troll under the bridge in Fremont, Seattle's guitar legend in Capitol Hill, a storied totem pole in Pioneer Square.
- Architecture enthusiasts will delight in the first skyscraper on the west coast, Smith Tower, the futuristic Central Library, or the magnificent glass Spheres filled with lush botanicals.
- For a bit of exercise try kayaking on Lake Union, jogging around Green Lake's paved path, or biking on the Burke-Gilman Trail starting at the beaches of Golden Gardens Park.
- Explore public spaces and encounter a gigantic Hat n' Boots at Oxbow Park, swim in the unique saltwater of Coleman Pool at Lincoln Park, or find words of inspiration along the terraced walls of the Martin Luther King, Jr. Civil Rights Memorial Park.
- If you're in need of locally made crafts or farm fresh produce and meat, look no further than the year-round University District Farmers' Market or one of the fifteen other neighborhood markets in town.
- Craving rubber chicken instead? Then a stop by Archie McPhee in Wallingford should do the trick.
- If you have extra time for a day trip, take a ferry to one of the many islands surrounding Seattle to enjoy the natural beauty of the region.

Whether you have a whole vacation or just a day to explore Seattle, your options are limitless. We included a few of our favorite places here to use as starting points, but encourage you to explore further – look around the corner, try a new food, or learn some local history along the way. One final insider's tip, Seattle is *not* the rainiest city in the US by a long shot, but if it does rain, locals don't use umbrellas.

Happy Exploring and Welcome to Seattle!

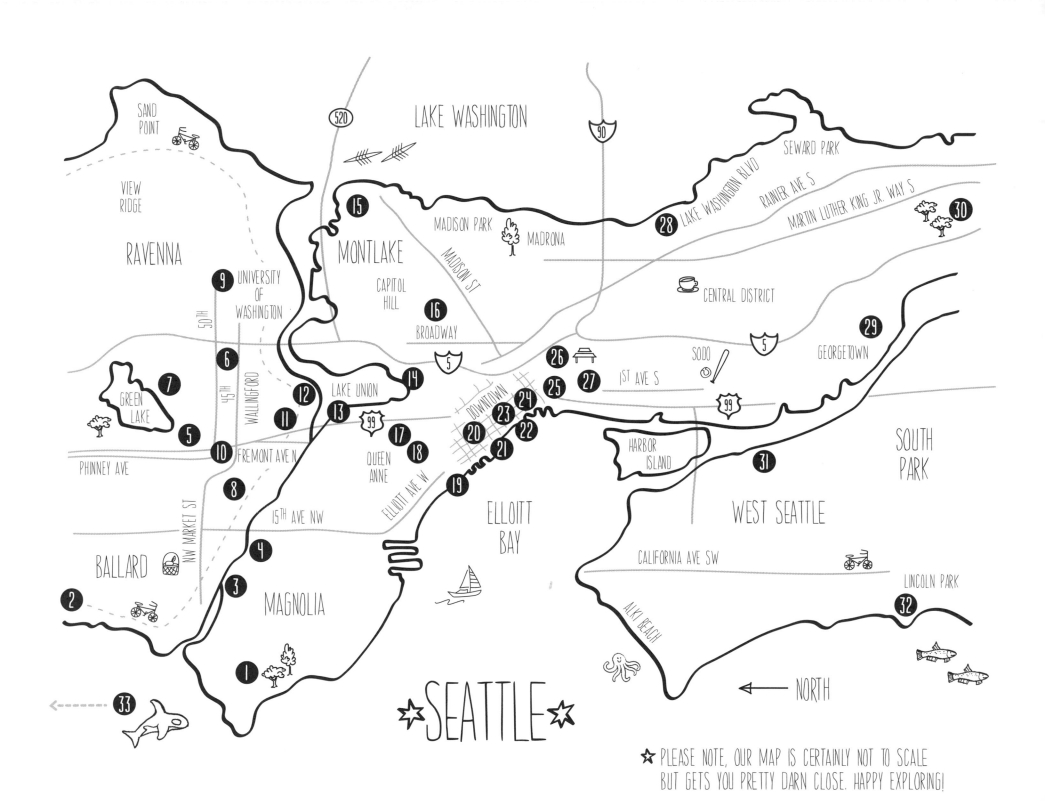

SAND POINT

VIEW RIDGE

RAVENNA

520

LAKE WASHINGTON

90

SEWARD PARK

LAKE WASHINGTON BLVD

RAINIER AVE S

MARTIN LUTHER KING JR. WAY S

30

28

MADISON PARK

MADRONA

MADISON ST

MONTLAKE

15

9 UNIVERSITY OF WASHINGTON

50TH

CAPITOL HILL

CENTRAL DISTRICT

16 BROADWAY

6

29

GEORGETOWN

45TH

7

WALLINGFORD

14

26

SODO

5

GREEN LAKE

12

LAKE UNION

27

1ST AVE S

99

25

5

11

13

DOWNTOWN

24

23

99

5

10 FREMONT AVE N

99

17

20 22

PHINNEY AVE

18

QUEEN ANNE

21

HARBOR ISLAND

SOUTH PARK

8

31

NW MARKET ST

4

15TH AVE NW

ELLIOTT AVE W

19

WEST SEATTLE

BALLARD

ELLIOTT BAY

CALIFORNIA AVE SW

3

MAGNOLIA

LINCOLN PARK

ALKI BEACH

32

1

33

← NORTH

☆ SEATTLE ☆

☆ PLEASE NOTE, OUR MAP IS CERTAINLY NOT TO SCALE BUT GETS YOU PRETTY DARN CLOSE. HAPPY EXPLORING!

COLORFUL SEATTLE LOCATIONS

Please note the information was correct at the time of publication, but as with all things in life it is subject to change. Happy exploring!

ART & ARCHITECTURE

19 The **Olympic Sculpture Park** is a vibrant green space, which connects the city to the Puget Sound, allowing visitors to experience a variety of unique sculptures in an outdoor setting. Jaume Plensa's "Echo" is named for the mountain nymph of Greek mythology, and is situated along the shoreline of the park looking across the Puget Sound to Mount Olympus. The park is open year-round and admission is free. • seattlemuseum.org

20 At the center of the Amazon campus, located in the South Lake Union neighborhood, sit three spectacular glass and steel spheres filled with lush tropical plantings. For a refreshing change from the office, employees are welcome to work surrounded by nature. More than 1,000 cloud forest species from around the world make up the biodiversity of **The Spheres**. Free public tours are available via appointment. • seattlespheres.com

3 Located in the heart of downtown, discover books in the stunning 11-story steel and glass **Seattle Public Central Library**, designed by world-renowned architects, Rem Koolhaas and Joshua Prince-Ramus. The "book spiral", four floors connected by ramps, creates an innovative space to house books. Read and peruse books in these great public spaces and don't miss the creative gift shop on level 3. • spl.org

24 **Smith Tower** has been an iconic fixture of the Seattle skyline for over a century. Built in 1914, it was the tallest building west of the Mississippi River. Explore Smith Tower's historical exhibits and enjoy 360-degree views of the city from the 35th floor Observatory Restaurant & Bar. Visit smithtower.com for tickets.

CITY PARKS

1 At over 530 acres, Magnolia's **Discovery Park** is Seattle's largest city park, consisting of two miles of protected tidal beaches, open meadows, dramatic sea cliffs, active sand dunes, and the historic West Point Lighthouse. A selection of great hikes make you feel as if you are not within the city. • seattle.gov/parks

2 Located in Ballard on the shores of the Puget Sound, **Golden Gardens Park** features one of Seattle's favorite sandy beaches, offering extraordinary views of the Olympic Mountains. Firepits are available for summer gatherings after a rousing game of beach volleyball. seattle.gov/parks

? Run, paddle, scull, walk, trot, or swim -- there are so many fun ways to get around — or across — **Green Lake Park**, hidden in the heart of several dense urban neighborhoods, and a stone's throw from the Woodland Park Zoo. Boat rentals available, and pickleball courts nearby. • seattle.gov/parks

12 Listed on the National Register of Historic Places, **Gas Works Park**, on Lake Union, beautifully integrates the remnants of the old gasification machinery with 19 acres of green space. It's absolutely the easiest place to fly a kite, and offers amazing views of the city skyline at sunset. • seattle.gov/parks

15 The **Washington Park Arboretum**, located along the shores of Lake Washington, offers 230 acres of wandering among a vast collection of botanical species. The 3.8-mile loop trail is a great escape in the middle of the city. If you're visiting in springtime, make sure to enjoy the colorful rhododendrons, and if in autumn, the grove of Japanese maples is sure to impress. Explore the northern portion of the park via canoe or kayak with reasonable rentals from the University of Washington. • seattle.gov/parks

26 A red pagoda, a life-size chess set, and many welcoming benches make **Hing Hay Park**, "The Park for Pleasurable Gatherings," a central meeting place in the International District. There are plenty of restaurants and cafes in the neighborhood for a lunchtime stop. seattle.gov/parks

29 A gigantic pair of "Hat n' Boots" is probably the craziest view from the top of any playground tower. This supersized sculpture was created in 1953 for a western-style gas station in the Georgetown neighborhood, and now resides a few streets away at **Oxbow Park**. seattle.gov/parks

30 Tucked away in South Seattle, **Kubota Garden** blends Japanese garden concepts — streams, waterfalls, ponds, and rock formations - with native Northwest plants. Started by Fujitaro Kubota in 1923, without any formal gardening training, it grew over the years to a stunning 20-acre landscape. The garden is open year-round and admission is free. kubotagarden.org

32 **Colman Pool** is a true hidden gem, located in a corner of West Seattle's waterfront Lincoln Park. In the summer months, this heated saltwater pool allows swimmers to take in views of the Puget Sound and neighboring Vashon Island. Enjoy miles of great trails, both in the trees and along the shore. • seattle.gov/parks

DAY TRIP

22 The **Washington State Ferries** system is the largest in the United States, serving 20 terminals which stretch from Vashon Island in the Puget Sound to British Columbia, Canada. More than 22 million riders each year use the fleet of 22 ferries to travel throughout the Pacific Northwest. Keep your eyes out for seals or orcas that occasionally ride alongside. • wsdot.wa.gov/ferries

33 Whidbey Island is easily accessible by ferry just north of the city. Drive up the island, stopping at beaches and quaint towns. At the top find **Deception Pass State Park** with exceptional hikes, massive cedar trees, and a breathtaking bridge connecting Whidbey to Fidalgo Island. Don't forget to eat some mussels in Coupeville on beautiful Penn Cove. parks.wa.gov

EATING & SHOPPING

6 Magic tricks, whoopee cushions, and the essential rubber chickens – so much nuttiness can be found at this purveyor of wacky novelties, **Archie McPhee**. No visit is possible without a belly-rolling laugh or two. See if you can find a yodeling pickle, Bigfoot socks, unicorn heads, and racing cats. • mcphee.com

9 From White Center in the south, to Broadview in the north, find local, farm fresh produce and artisan food products at 15 neighborhood farmers markets across Seattle. The **University District Farmers Market** is one of six year-round markets. seattlefarmersmarket.org

EXPLORABLE HISTORY

4 Located between Ballard and Magnolia, **Fishermen's Terminal** is home to hundreds of working fishing boats that spend months on the open sea off the coast of Washington, Canada, and Alaska. Walk through the array of colorful boats, stop for a cup of chowder, or buy fresh seafood at the market along the entrance. • portseattle.org

14 The **Center for Wooden Boats** is not a typical maritime museum. Hands-on experiences are encouraged through the repair or rental of its fleet of historic wooden boats. The floating boathouses are designated Seattle Historic Landmarks, and are adjacent to Lake Union Park. • cwb.org

28 **Martin Luther King, Jr. Civil Rights Memorial Park** is designed around a granite 'mountain' inspired by the "I've Been to the Mountaintop" speech given in 1968. The City of Seattle added "Civil Rights" to the park's name to acknowledge community leaders who work on social justice issues. Take time to read the inspirational plaques or walk the terraces for stunning views of downtown Seattle from its Central District location. seattle.gov/parks

31 The **Duwamish Longhouse and Cultural Center** is the home of the Duwamish people which serves as a tribal headquarters and education center. With its large cedar posts and surrounding benches, the Longhouse, is the center of social and ceremonial meetings for the tribe. The intricate floor mosaic of cedar tiles shows the Duwamish Tribe's physical location between the Olympic and Cascade Mountain ranges. Free admission. duwamishtribe.org

OUTDOOR ADVENTURES

Visit the Fish Ladder at the **Hiram M. Chittenden Locks** in the Ballard neighborhood to see salmon travel its 21 steps as they swim upstream from the Puget Sound to spawn in the many rivers and streams of Washington. Be sure to stop at the Salmon Education Center to learn about their amazing journey. To access the fish ladder, walk over the locks, but make sure to watch the frenetic activity as vessels of all sizes navigate the transition from fresh to salt water. • ballardlocks.org

5 Naturally inspiring and multi-award winning, the **Woodland Park Zoo** is dedicated to conservation and education, while simultaneously providing care for nearly 1,100 animals representing over 300 different species. So many animals to explore from the supersized Komodo dragon to the whimsical penguin colony. • zoo.org

8 The **Burke-Gilman Trail** starts on the shores of Ballard and extends east 20 miles along Lake Washington to Bothell where it meets the Sammamish River Trail. Its smooth, flat path is ideal for walkers, runners, cyclists, and skaters alike. Many stops along the trail offer resting points or a bite to eat. • seattle.gov/parks

13 Situated in the heart of Seattle and home to countless houseboats, **Lake Union** connects the Puget Sound to Lake Washington, and is the city's water hotspot for floatplane departures, working tugboat sightings, and paddling kayakers. Don't miss Tuesday night "Duck Dodge" race in summer where sailboats of any size and crew compete.

15 **Pioneer Square** marks Seattle's original downtown, dating back to 1852. 'Seattle Totem Pole' made by the Tlinglit people, historically known as the 'Chief-of-All-Women Pole', is the focal point of the neighborhood. Explore this area for interesting galleries and unique shops. • pioneersquare.org

SPECTACULAR SCULPTURES

10 Who says trolls don't live under bridges? In Seattle they do! Four local artists created the **Fremont Troll** in an effort to clean up the space under the Aurora Bridge. Visitors are encouraged to climb, explore, and gaze into the troll's one good eye - a hubcap! fremont.com

11 Often creatively decorated with personal messages for celebratory events by local residents, the Fremont sculpture, **Waiting for the Interurban**, commemorates a bygone train that used to connect the neighborhood to downtown. • fremont.com

16 The life like bronze statue of Seattle native **Jimi Hendrix** resides in the Capitol Hill neighborhood and commemorates one of rock music's most influential guitarists. Wander around to find an eclectic range of restaurants, music venues, and coffee shops.

ENTERTAINMENT & SPORTS

17 Few buildings require a perimeter walk to gaze at the creative energy prior to entry. This one certainly does. Designed by Frank Gehry, **MoPOP** — The Museum of Pop Culture, is a cutting-edge, nonprofit museum, dedicated to popular culture as seen in science fiction, TV, and music. Don't miss the extensive guitar collection from many rock and roll legends. mopop.org

18 The 605-foot-tall **Space Needle**, built for the 1962 World's Fair, is Seattle's most famous landmark and offers fantastic views of the city and beyond. Tickets are available for the Observation Deck and The Loupe, a rotating glass floor. • spaceneedle.com

21 **The Seattle Great Wheel**, found on Pier 57 on the waterfront, is one of the largest Ferris wheels on the West Coast. Its 42 gondolas offer breathtaking views of the city and water from their perch high above Elliott Bay. • seattlegreatwheel.com

27 Located in SoDo, the multi-purpose stadium, **Lumen Field**, is home to the Seattle Seahawks (NFL), Seattle Sounders (MLS), and OL Reign (NWSL). Don't forget your scarf or jersey! lumenfield.com

NOTES:

DISCOVERY PARK

CHITTENDEN LOCKS FISH LADDER

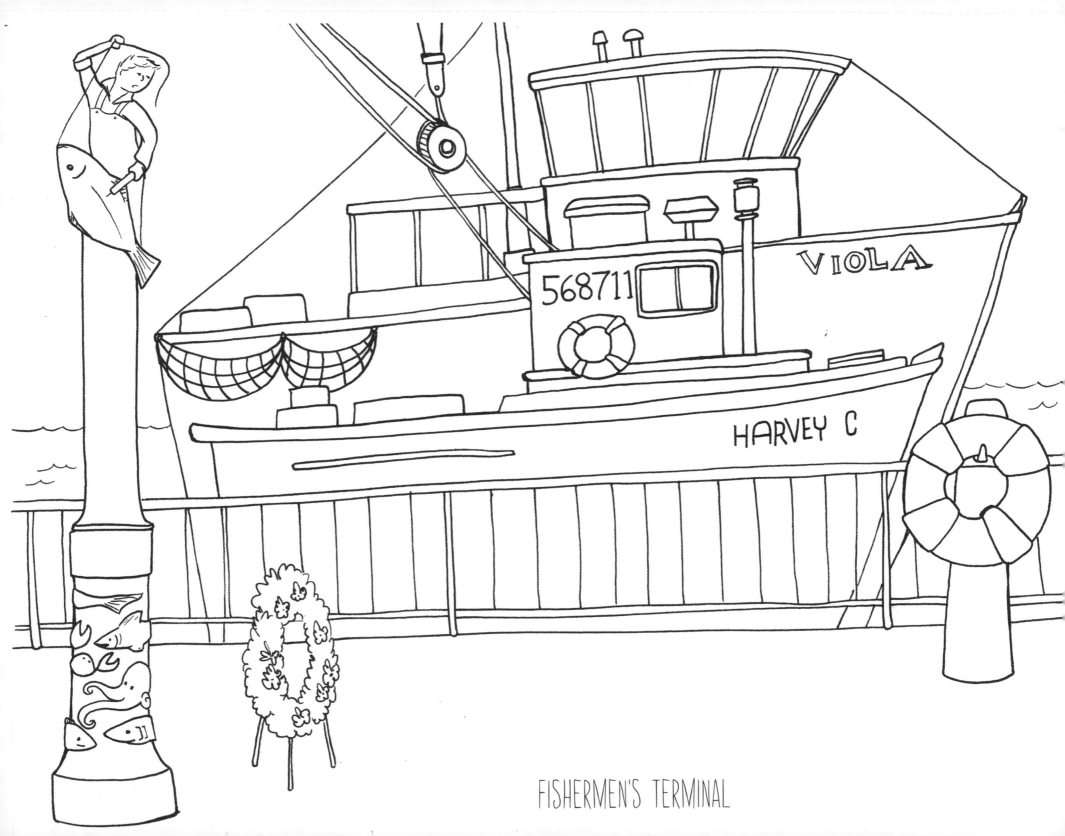

FISHERMEN'S TERMINAL

WOODLAND PARK ZOO

GREEN LAKE PARK

BURKE-GILMAN TRAIL

To Magnuson Park
To Kenmore

USE BELL
OR VOICE
WHEN
PASSING

FREMONT TROLL

WAITING FOR THE INTERURBAN SCULPTURE

GAS WORKS PARK

LAKE UNION

THE CENTER FOR WOODEN BOATS

WASHINGTON PARK ARBORETUM

JIMI HENDRIX STATUE

MUSEUM
OF
POP
CULTURE
MoPoP.org

SPACE NEEDLE

OLYMPIC SCULPTURE PARK

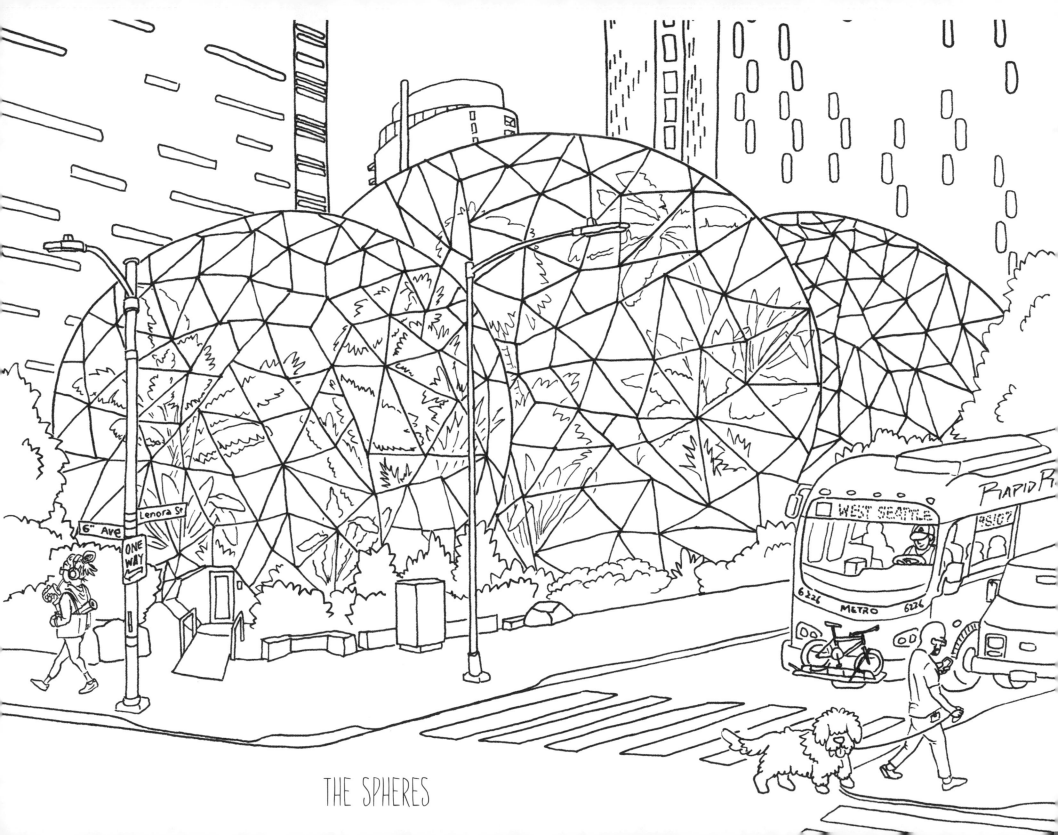

THE SPHERES

THE SEATTLE GREAT WHEEL

WASHINGTON STATE FERRIES

CENTRAL LIBRARY

SMITH TOWER

PIONEER SQUARE

浩然亭

HING HAY PARK

LUMEN FIELD

MARTIN LUTHER KING, JR. CIVIL RIGHTS MEMORIAL PARK

OXBOW PARK

DUWAMISH LONGHOUSE

DECEPTION PASS STATE PARK